*Martial Arts
History, Forms and Techniques
Volume Five*

Buddha Crane Karate
The First Matrixed Art

Al Case

AL CASE

Quality Press

Copyright© 2024 by Alton H. Case

All rights reserved. No part of this book may be reproduced or transmitted in any form or by any means, electronic or mechanical, including photocopying, recording, or by any information storage and retrieval system, without the written permission of the author.

For information regarding this book go to:
MonsterMartialArts.com
or
AlCaseBooks.com

AUTHOR'S NOTE

Take Karate a small nibble at a time and after a few years you will have eaten the entire menu and be 'Karate fat' for the rest of your life. the trick is to make sure that you set aside a few minutes every day and practice. You don't have to work yourself into a frothy sweat. You don't have to grind yourself into a pulp. What you do have to do is look, understand, do, and let the results accumulate. this can be done easily if you just persist. To emphasize, the most important thing is understanding.

AL CASE

TABLE OF CONTENTS

introduction	7
1) Buddha Crane Karate	9
2) The Eight Basic Blocks	11
3) A Circle of Blocks	12
4) More About Basics	13
5) Body Testing	15
6) The Lines	16
7) The Buddha Palm	17
8) Line One	19
9) CBM	22
10) Line Two	23
11) The three Levels of the Martial Arts	26
12) Line Three	27
13) The Three Essential Ingredients	30
14) Line Four	31
15) How the Art Becomes Untrue	34
16) Line Five	35
17) The Secret of Internal Energy	41
18) Line Six	42
19) The Ten Arm Positions	48
20) Line Seven	49
21) The Seven Directions	55
22) Line Eight	56
23) Cutting the Art Down to Size	62
24) Line Nine ~ the Sword Catcher	63
25) How to Preserve the True Art	67
26) Line Ten ~ The Foot Catcher	68
27) A Shameless Ad	72
28) Line Eleven ~ Rolling Backfist	73
29) Fighting	79
30) Line Twelve ~ Falling Crane	80
31) More About Fighting	86
32) Line Thirteen ~ Dart	87
33) The Most About Fighting	92
34) Line Fourteen ~ Hammer	93
35) The Geometry of the Arts	100

36) House 101
37) Two Man House 104
38) Moon 106
39) The Vision of the White Crane 112
40) The Secret of the White Crane 125
41) Extra Applications 127
42) The Final Word 134

INTRODUCTION

Students come in many attitudes.

There is the child who wishes to make pilgrimage to the sacred mountain and study at the foot of the master. Quite honestly, this is usually a fantasy, and this type of student normally doesn't last long. Fantasy is not a good foundation for an Art that requires patience and enduring work over long periods of time. Passion may be admirable, but it means nothing without guts and fortitude.

There is the fellow who wishes to learn to fight. He lasts for a while, but eventually falls by the way. While there is an Art to fighting, fighting is not the Art. the Art requires a person to evolve as a human being.

And then there is the fellow who applies himself without much talk, who works hard, year after year, never questioning, never asking why, never being seduced by things such as fame, money, and other fleeting desires.

These are the people who make the best students.

Why? Because they decided to be Artists.

An Artist is a superior human being.

Man is superior to animal merely because he can deal in Abstract thought.

An Artist's whole being is preoccupied with Abstract thought. He lives, quite honestly, in another realm. He stands before you, and yet he is not of you. He is somewhere else. He is somewhere abstract. He leads the way into the other realms.

He does not stand in the rear and point the way.

He breaks trail and fights the battles which guide and shape the Universe.

What we are talking about is a concern for Art that overrides comfort, the need for money, the foolish desire to beat up your fellow man, self~image, mysticism, and so on.

If there is a phrase that describes us it is Silent Zealots. People who know me call me a fanatic.

That is good.

Let's talk about this book.

to understand this book you should understand the frustration out of which it was born.

Karate, currently, is taught by people preoccupied with translating the shadow of Art into bucks. I see children being taught to 'Get the point.' I see Art betrayed by inadequate methodology, which methodology is foisted upon human beings by brain bound idiots who pretend to be Artists.

Actually, the Art is proof against idiots. One could take almost any Art, even the ones taught by idiots, and, by performing a few analytical feats, discover the true Art.

The problem is that one has to be willing and able to rearrange and make usable vast amounts of data.

This book will help you do that.

Before I close let me make a point. To succeed at Karate, or any other Martial Art, one needs three things: A good Art, a good teacher, and a good student.

There is a good Art in these pages. I am a good teacher.

Are you a good student?

1
BUDDHA~CRANE KARATE

In the Introduction I made reference to a few problems which plague the Arts on the whole. Let me get a little more specific.

Basics are not understood as they relate to the physics of planet Earth and the bodies which move around on the planet.

Techniques have become unrealistic and unworkable. the entire realm of technique is a bastard which has thrown a random assortment of tricks into a bag and mixed them up.

Forms are not anything like fighting, do not scientifically develop Classical Power, and so on.

Arts have become repositories for outdated methods which were developed for entirely different circumstances than would be encountered today.

The entire methodology of teaching has become an inadequate 'Monkey see~monkey do' process through which no real information is given.

Generally speaking, the Arts being taught as Karate do not develop Artists. People are not trained to actively think within the chaos of actual combat, and they are not trained to create technique upon the moment and as the need arrives.

And then there is Buddha Crane. Let me explain just a bit of why and how it has solved the problems just mentioned.

Data was resolved until there was an empirical process which worked one hundred per cent of the time, and which developed Classical Power in the student.

Basics were resolved until there were only eight Karate Blocks which surrounded the body in a circle. this gave a strong foundation which was true to the principle of Karate meeting Force with Force, and which allowed for future development.

Techniques were resolved, and the eight Basics were examined until they could be gathered in eight 'Lines.' These lines presented the most realistic techniques possible in Karate, and these techniques, when understood, can be combined in various fashion to create combinations and other techniques. Forms were ignored except as exercises through which the student can create his own concepts of body motion and combat.

And the whole thing makes sense.

Sometimes I had to be brutal in my deletions to accepted method.

Sometimes I had to be creative. Sometimes I had to borrow from other methodologies to reorganize the beast that Karate had become.

Ultimately, if you do the Art as I have presented it in these pages, you will find something that is true. It is simple and easy to learn, and yet can be developed into other Arts as the student progresses to that need.

Buddha refers to perfection of method and Art which you will find here.

Crane refers to balance and grace and the soaring of artistic imaginations.

And it all relies on you. Can you be true?

2
THE EIGHT BASIC BLOCKS

HIGH CROSSED WRIST BLOCK
HIGH BLOCK
UPPER CROSS PALM BLOCK
KNIFE BLOCK
MIDDLE BLOCK
LOWER CROSS PALM BLOCK
LOW BLOCK
LOW CROSSED WRIST BLOCK

3
A CIRCLE OF BLOCKS

This diagram represents the specific blocking arrangement of the arms. Imagine the circle in the center as the body to be protected, and the lines surrounding it as the specific angles of the blocks. Each block protects roughly a 'Hand' of area on the circle. The Middle Block can be done inward or outward. the Knife block is usually done diagonally and downward. thus the two right angle diagonals are the same position with different geometries. Actually, any block can utilize any geometry in finding it's classical position, but we are just looking at the fixed position geometry of the arms.

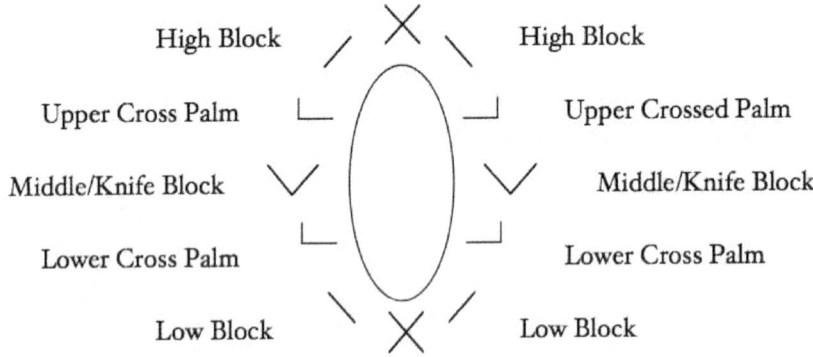

Of course there are many deviations and variations of these blocks and the methods of their execution.

4
MORE ABOUT THE BASICS

The Low Block has a hidden Upper Cross Palm Block as it circles in front of the face. Remember to drop the entire body weight into the block.

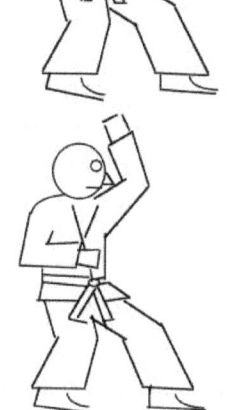

The High Block starts as an Uppercut in line from the Energy Center (tan tien). Breath out when you expand, Breath in when you contract.

Step off line of attack and rotate the hips to execute this block. the secret is in the line from the fist to the tan tien.

Rotate diagonal (past the ear) and down to combine from both hip rotation and gravity for maximum power. An Iron Rod of Energy in the arm.

The Upper Cross Palm protects the face. Create a 'Box' of right angles with the arm and direct the power around the shoulders and down.

The Lower Cross Palm creates a 'Box' in which the palm protects the body. Turn the body but keep an 'Energy line' from the wrist to the back foot.

Cross the wrists. This is the 'Sword Catcher' block. Control the distance between bodies and you will understand.

Cross the wrists. This is the 'Foot Catcher' block. This block may be used for virtually any kick.

5
BODY TESTING

Body Testing is crucial to developing the True Art because the True Art hinges upon the body being attached firmly to the ground. Let me rant and rave about this for a moment.

The body is a machine. The legs are used to bolt the machine down, and the Tan Tien ('The One Point' located some two inches below the navel) is the generator of Energy. Stances are used to keep the body attached to the ground and the flow of Energy high. The lower the stance the more work one has to perform, the more Energy one has. In combat, of course, one must find the medium which includes both mobility and solidity. In training, however, this can be taken to extremes. The point of all this is this: To help in structural alignment, attachment of the body machine to the planet, and other things necessary to the definition of the word True (look it up in the dictionary if you want to truly understand the concept of a 'True Art'). In Art one should utilize the concept of Body Testing to the maximum.

When Body Testing the Instructor pushes on the stance so that the Force is conducted through the body to the ground.

The easier it is for the student to resist the better his Art.

The Instructor must know exactly how to push so that student learns how to use less and less resistance. This is an exact science.

6
THE LINES

When one learns any method of communication, and Art, above all, is communication, that communication must take on a certain form. There are letters, words and sentences. In the Martial Arts the individual basic move is a letter. When basics are put together they form a technique, or word.

The following 'Lines' are the Eight Words necessary to understanding True Karate.

They are lines because they are done on a line. One may do a couple of moves in one direction and then return, or hundreds of moves in one direction, and then return. The idea of putting the 'Words' together in lines came to me from examining the way Ton Toi (Northern Shaolin Kung Fu ~ 'Springy Legs') and Pa Kua Chang (Internal Kung Fu ~'Eight Trigrams Palm Maneuvers') were taught. Interestingly, I had to throw away a lot of Karate lines such as Three Step Blocking. The reason was that they were just letters being repeated, not letters combined into words.

This idea of the lines being small Karate words is important. You will find, as you do the lines, that they are little techniques which use just the basic eight 'Letters.' Doing them is like a child with blocks learning how to spell 'Cat,' or 'Dog.' You could expand upon these words and learn how to spell 'Catatonic,' or 'Dogmatic,' but these small words are much, much more important than any other words you will ever come up with. The reason is because they work. Larger words usually don't work. I'm not saying you shouldn't learn how to spell 'Catatonic,' or 'Dogmatic.' I'm just saying that a person who knows how to say 'Eat,' or 'Work,' can live better in a foreign land than somebody who can say 'Cataclysmic.'

Think about this as you practice the lines. Master them and create whole sentences (Forms) and stories (Arts), but remember to speak simply to fools. It is the best way to survive.

7
THE BUDDHA PALM

The Buddha Palm block is a Cross Palm Block with one hand while the other hand is held below the elbow, as if cupping the elbow. This block is crucial to the Buddha Crane system, and has the potential to change the way you think about Karate.

If somebody strikes at you your initial instinctive action is to slap the strike away. So why fight it? Why fight your initial reaction? Why try to change this reaction? If it is what you do then trust it and work on it until it works. Then this initial reaction can lead into the rest of Karate. If somebody strikes you instinctively slap at it, letting your body assume the Buddha Palm block, then your training in the lines can take over and you can apply effective Karate technique. This way you will avoid trying to undo instinctive reactions, which are natural, and make them work for you. This is a much more logical approach to the Art of Self Defense.

There is another reason for the Buddha Palm Block, however.

What is this? If you have a quick mental you can tell that it is two words. The words are:

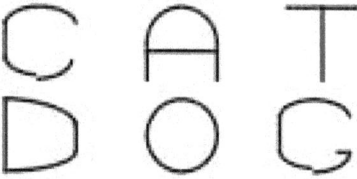

The reason they are hard to understand in the first example is because they are overlapped. They are overlapped because there was no space between the words. Thus letters mush together and are hard to distinguish and, if it was a Karate word, it would lose it's focus and become some form of Mush Do.

The point I am making is that the Buddha Palm is the space between words, and even letters. Properly done the Buddha Palm Block makes each word understandable and communicable.

Improperly done and you have mush.

And here is something you should know, beyond just the linguistic
aspects, about the True Art of Karate. The word Karate means 'Empty hands.' Empty has to do with the concept of 'Space.'

What I am saying is that the secret of Karate is not the Energy, it is the space between the Energy .

A candle during the daytime has not much effect. A candle at night has great effect.

Why? Because of the space around the candle.

And you must create space around your technique...and the individual letters of your technique.

Understanding the Buddha Palm Block will help you do this.

When you see the Buddha Palm Block realize that you are not seeing focus. You are seeing space between focus, between basic and technique. Even if the Buddha Palm is stopped, it is space.

If you understand this one point your Buddha Palm will shine, and you will master the Art rapidly .

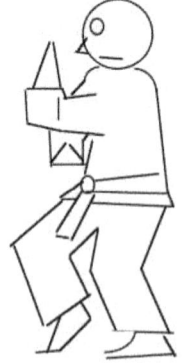
Buddha Palm from side
(Cat Stance)

Buddha Palm from front
(Horse Stance)

8
LINE ONE

1) Step back with the right foot to a Cat Stance as you execute a right Buddha Palm Block.

2) Step forward with the left foot to a Toe Up Back Stance as you execute a left Low Block.

3) Shift forward to a Front Stance as you execute a right Punch.

4) Step forward with the right foot to a Cat Stance as you execute a left Buddha Palm Block.

5) Step forward with the right foot to a Toe Up Back Stance as you execute a right Low Block.

6) Shift forward to a Front Stance as you execute a left Punch.

7) Step forward with the left foot to a Cat Stance as you execute a right Buddha Palm Block.

8) Step forward with the left foot to a Toe Up Back Stance as you execute a left Low Block.

9) Shift forward to a Front Stance as you execute a right Punch.

10) Step back with the left foot and face to the right in an Hourglass Stance as you execute a left Buddha Palm Block.

Pivot to the right and do the form in the opposite direction.

Special note:

It may seem strange to assume the Toe Up Back Stance while you block, but this move balances the explosion coming from the Tan Tien. You can use the Heel Stomp during Self Defense, or use the block with a normal Back Stance, and so on.

APPLICATION ONE

9
CBM

CBM stands for 'Coordinated Body Motion.' It is:

'When all part of the body support One Intention'

What this means is that the structure must be aligned from ground to target. The breathing must be done in conjunction with the expansion and contraction of the body. All body parts must start motion at the same time...and stop motion at the same time. The motion of all body parts must take into account relative weight, mass, potential geometries of motion, and so on and so on.

In short, all pieces of the body must be analyzed as to how they can move in concert with the whole body .

In other words, you must use the body as One Unit.

When the body moves as One Unit, when it CBMs, Intention will manifest. When Intention is unleashed the True Art may begin.

10
LINE TWO

1) Step back with the right foot to a Cat Stance as you execute a right Buddha Palm Block (Left wrist dangles).

2) Step forward with the left foot to a Toe Up Back Stance as you execute a left Outward Block.

3) Shift forward to a Front Stance as you execute a right Punch.

4) Step forward with the right foot to a Cat Stance as you execute a left Buddha Palm Block (right wrist dangles).

5) Step forward with the right foot to a Toe Up Back Stance as you execute a right Outward Block.

6) Shift forward to a Front Stance as you execute a left Punch.

7) Step forward with the left foot to a Cat Stance as you execute a right Buddha Palm Block (left wrist dangles).

8) Step forward with the left foot to a Toe Up Back Stance as you execute a left Outward Block.

BUDDHA CRANE KARATE

9) Shift forward to a Front Stance as you execute a right Punch.

10) Step back with the left foot and face to the right in an Hourglass Stance as you execute a left Buddha Palm Block.
Pivot to the right and do the form in the opposite direction.

Special note:

Hold the blocking arm up if necessary while punching. It is easy to change these basics into simultaneous block and strikes.

APPLICATION TWO

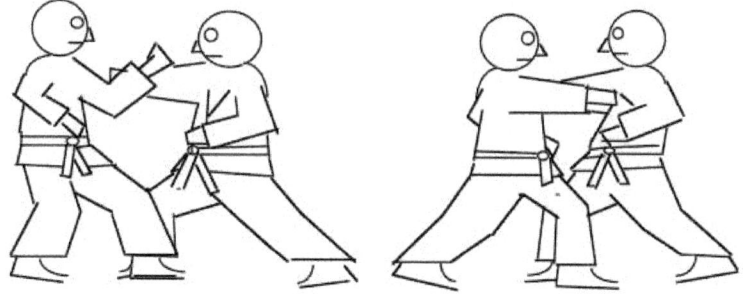

11
THE THREE LEVELS OF THE MARTIAL ARTS

The Three Levels of the Martial Arts are:

Mechanics	Structure	Control own body
		Control Force with Force
Physics	Energy	Control own mind
		Control another's body
		Control Force with Flow
Dynamics	Thought	Control own Spirit
		Control another's mind
		Control Flow with Flow

When one CBMs he is able to move into controlling Force with Flow. This is a Black Belt.

When one moves into the Third Level one is a Master. This is a Fourth Degree Black Belt

12
LINE THREE

1) Step back with the right foot to a Cat Stance as you execute a right Buddha Palm Block.

2) Step forward with the left foot to a Toe Up Back Stance as you execute a left High Block.

3) Shift forward to a Front Stance as you execute a right Punch.

4) Step forward with the right foot to a Cat Stance as you execute a left Buddha Palm Block.

5) Step forward with the right foot to a Toe Up Back Stance as you execute a right High Block.

6) Shift forward to a Front Stance as you execute a left Punch.

7) Step forward with the left foot to a Cat Stance as you execute a right Buddha Palm Block (left wrist dangles).

8) Step forward with the left foot to a Toe Up Back Stance as you execute a left High Block.

9) Shift forward to a Front Stance as you execute a right Punch.

10) Step back with the left foot and face to the right in an Hourglass Stance as you execute a left Buddha Palm Block.

Pivot to the right and do the form in the opposite direction.

Special note:

Always look at the eyes. The eyes are the windows to the soul. Look through the eyes to the spirit and see the Thought behind the Action.

APPLICATION THREE

13
THE THREE ESSENTIAL INGREDIENTS

The Three Essential Ingredients of the Martial Arts are:

Forms   Self Defense   Freestyle

A Form is theory.
Self Defense moves are how the theory might be translated into reality. Freestyle is the ultimate translation of theory and self~defense into reality.
A Form is incredibly important because when you practice the Martial Arts you must learn to control your own 'Form.'
Self~defense is incredibly important because one is taught how to control somebody else's 'Form.' This is accomplished with the help of a partner.
Freestyle is incredibly important because one learns how to control somebody else's Form without their help.

The important item, behind all this, is that the Art is about Control.
Control yourself, control others, control the Art on all Three Levels. Learn this and you will learn that the True Art is not about fighting at all. It is about understanding the component parts of a fight until there is no mystery, and there is no fight, and there is only scientific evaluation.
And it all starts with a sincere study of Forms, Self~Defense and Freestyle.

14
LINE FOUR

1) Step back with the right foot to a Cat Stance as you execute a right Buddha Palm Block.

2) Step forward with the left foot to a Toe Up Back Stance as you execute a left Diagonal Knife Block.

3) Shift forward to a Front Stance as you execute a right Punch.

4) Step forward with the right foot to a Cat Stance as you execute a left Buddha Palm Block .

5) Step forward with the right foot to a Toe Up Back Stance as you execute a right Diagonal Knife Block.

6) Shift forward to a Front Stance as you execute a left Punch.

7) Step forward with the left foot to a Cat Stance as you execute a right Buddha Palm Block.

8) Step forward with the left foot to a Toe Up Back Stance as you execute a left Diagonal Knife Block.

BUDDHA CRANE KARATE

9) Shift forward to a Front Stance as you execute a right Punch.

10) Step back with the left foot and face to the right in an Hourglass Stance as you execute a left Buddha Palm Block.

Pivot to the right and do the form in the opposite direction.

Special note:

Imagine there is an iron bar in your forearm.

APPLICATION FOUR

15
HOW THE ART BECOMES UNTRUE

True, according to the dictionary, means 'Consistent with fact or reality.

Also, and this is important, 'Proper alignment or adjustment.'

So many people sign up for a course of instruction because of the fantasy provoked by movies and advertising.

When they begin their instruction they are told that this technique is deadly and this technique will do this and...and it's usually all just more of the hype that got them into the studio in the first place.

Salesmen selling to make sure the buyer keeps buying.

What is 'True' is what 'Works.'

So the student has to throw out fantasy. The best way to do this is to understand the concept of 'Body Testing,' which I described earlier in this tome.

Find what works. Find the proper alignment within your body so that the body can support the generation of your own Force, or resist the introduction of outside Force to you.

This is what will make your Art, or any Art, for that matter, 'True.'

It takes work and honesty .

It does not take fantasy.

16
LINE FIVE

1) Step back with the right foot to a Cat Stance as you cross the wrists in front of the body with the palms up.

2) Step forward with the left foot to a Toe Up Back Stance as you execute a Double Low Block.

3) Retract the left foot to a Cat Stance as you execute a left Buddha Palm Block.

4) Execute a left Front Snap Kick.

5) Step forward with the left foot to a Toe Up Back Stance.

6) Shift forward into a Front Stance as you execute a right Punch.

7) Step forward with the right foot to a Cat Stance as you cross the wrists in front of the body with the palms up.

8) Step forward with the right foot to a Toe Up Back Stance as you execute a Double Low Block.

9) Retract the right foot to a Cat Stance as you execute a right Cross Palm Block.

10) Execute a right Front Snap Kick.

11) Step forward with the right foot to a Toe Up Back Stance.

12) Shift forward into a Front Stance as you execute a left Punch.

13) Step forward with the left foot to a Cat Stance as you cross the wrists in front of the body with the palms up.

14) Step forward with the left foot to a Toe Up Back Stance as you execute a Double Low Block.

15) Retract the left foot to a Cat Stance as you execute a left Buddha Palm Block.

16) Execute a left Front Snap Kick.

17) Step forward with the left foot to a Toe Up Back Stance.

18) Step forward with the left foot to a Front Stance as you execute a right Punch.

19) Step back with the left foot and face to the right in an Hourglass Stance as you execute a left Buddha Palm Block.

Pivot to the right and repeat the form in the opposite direction.

Special note:

Practice fast with focus. Practice slow as in Tai Chi. Fast for explosive power. Slow for Suspensive Strength. Backwards if you want to learn it faster.

APPLICATION FIVE

Raise the kicking knee, bend the support knee, drop the weight, tilt the hips, snap the foot as you would a fist to make a good Snap kick.

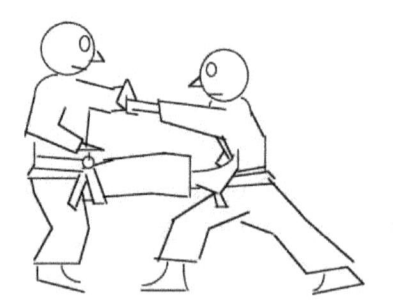

How would you use a double block to break a two handed push?

17
THE SECRET OF INTERNAL ENERGY

Internal Energy is Energy on the inside of the body.

Take a piece of pipe and half fill it with sand. Whenever you shake the pipe make sure the sand hits the wall all at once. If you shake the pipe endwise it is a punch or kick. If you shake it sideways it is a block. Always imagine your arms and legs as pipes filled with sand. In fact, you can actually imagine your whole body as nothing but a big pipe.

Sometimes people have a rough time getting the 'Pipe concept.' Another way of understanding this, or at least getting enough reality so it will make sense, is to dip your hands in a pail of water. Now do punches until they are dry. No quick shaking, nothing but technique and focus.

Though it is sometimes difficult getting into the idea of Internal Energy the above is a good introduction.

18
LINE SIX

1) Step back with the right foot to a Cat Stance as you cross the wrists in front of the hips with the palms down.

2) Step forward with the left foot to a Toe Up Back Stance as you execute a Double Outward Block.

3) Retract the left foot to a Cat Stance as you execute a left Buddha Palm Block.

4) Execute a left Front Snap Kick.

5) Step forward with the left foot to a Toe Up Back Stance.

6) Shift forward into a Front Stance as you execute a right Punch.

7) Step forward with the right foot to a Cat Stance as you cross the wrists in front of the hips with the palms down.

8) Step forward with the right foot to a Toe Up Back Stance as you execute a Double Outward Block.

9) Retract the right foot to a Cat Stance as you execute a right Cross Palm Block.

10) Execute a right Front Snap Kick.

11) Step forward with the right foot to a Toe Up Back Stance.

12) Shift forward into a Front Stance as you execute a left Punch.

13) Step forward with the left foot to a Cat Stance as you cross the wrists in front of the hips with the palms down.

14) Step forward with the left foot to a Toe Up Back Stance as you execute a Double Outward Block.

15) Retract the left foot to a Cat Stance as you execute a left Buddha Palm Block.

16) Execute a left Front Snap Kick.

17) Step forward with the left foot to a Toe Up Back Stance.

18) Step forward with the left foot to a Front Stance as you execute a right Punch.

19) Step back with the left foot and face to the right in an Hourglass Stance as you execute a left Buddha Palm Block.

Pivot to the right and repeat the form in the opposite direction.

Special note:

Never let the front knee, in a Front Stance, go beyond the heel or toe. The knee, heel and toe are the basis of an Energy triangle. Can you find the other triangles within karate?

APPLICATION SIX

Drop the weight, turn the support foot to commit the hips, use plant and push to increase leg strength.

Try stepping back into different stances when you do the kicks.

19
THE TEN ARM POSITIONS

When somebody starts a study of the Art they always say, or at least think, that their Art is best. It's basic loyalty. That's just the nature of man. And it can be taken to a fault.

Consider that there are only so many positions available to the arms, and there are only so many geometries.

One could define, literally , tens of thousands of techniques, but they are all the same, based upon the same basics, and those basics are virtually the same from Art to Art.

There are ten BAPs (Basic Arm Positions). They are the combinations of Low , Middle, High, and Across (Circular).

Karate likes to have the arm straight, depending upon Explosive Energy from the T an Tien.

Kung Fu likes variations on a curved Arm.

The real difference is going to be in the footwork. Put the 10 BAP into a Cross Step on a circle and you have Pa Kua. Put the 10 BAP on a line and you have Hsing I (Mind Form Boxing). Put the 10 BAP on a Two Step with a Flow and you have Aikido. Put the 10 BAP on random footwork with a hard Flow and you have Shaolin.

And so on and so on and so on.

The funny thing is when you tell somebody with many years invested in an Art about this and he'll nod his head, say 'Uh huh,' and keep right on going with what he is doing.

He doesn't want to change, and he won't change. Not because what I've said here is wrong, but because he's got too much time invested in his Art. In his mind he can't afford to change.

But all Arts really are nothing more than interchanges of footwork and the 10 BAP.

20
LINE SEVEN

1) Step back with the right foot to a Cat Stance as you cross the wrists in front of the body with the palms up.

2) Step forward with the left foot to a Toe Up Back Stance as you execute a Double High Block.

3) Retract the left foot to a Cat Stance as you execute a left Buddha Palm Block.

4) Execute a left Front Snap Kick.

5) Step forward with the left foot to a Toe Up Back Stance.

6) Shift forward into a Front Stance as you execute a right Punch.

7) Step forward with the right foot to a Cat Stance as you cross the wrists in front of the body with the palms up.

8) Step forward with the right foot to a Toe Up Back Stance as you execute a Double High Block.

9) Retract the right foot to a Cat Stance as you execute a right Cross Palm Block.

10) Execute a right Front Snap Kick.

11) Step forward with the right foot to a Toe Up Back Stance.

12) Shift forward into a Front Stance as you execute a left Punch.

13) Step forward with the left foot to a Cat Stance as you cross the wrists in front of the body with the palms up.

14) Step forward with the left foot to a Toe Up Back Stance as you execute a Double High Block.

15) Retract the left foot to a Cat Stance as you execute a left Buddha Palm Block.

16) Execute a left Front Snap Kick.

17) Step forward with the left foot to a Toe Up Back Stance.

18) Step forward with the left foot to a Front Stance as you execute a right Punch.

19) Step back with the left foot and face to the right in an Hourglass Stance as you execute a left Buddha Palm Block.

Pivot to the right and repeat the form in the opposite direction.

Special note:

You should practice Form when you are practicing applications, and practice applications when you are doing the Form. This will make your Theory work, and your work will be sound in theory.

APPLICATION SEVEN

Drop the weight, turn the support foot to commit the hips, use the kick like a hammer, not a bat.

Can you see how to destroy your opponent's stance with a kick?

21
THE SEVEN DIRECTIONS

Forward, back, left, right, up and down. These are the 'X, Y and Z' of Martial Motion. The Seventh Direction is just to stay in place.

There are seven potential directions for entering any of the 10 BAP.

Of course these are limited because certain of them don't work under Body Testing. And some are downright illogical because they break Economy of Motion (the least done for the most result).

For instance, the Middle Block.
1) Inward Block
2) Outward Block
3) Elbow Down
4) Uppercut
5) Pull (in)
6) Backfist (out)
7) Stay in place

So go ahead, examine each of the Four Basics, find the basic geometry to make it work. Now comes the fun part.

Take, for instance, the Low Block/Low Block. There are 49 ways (7 x's 7) to enter this BAP. Times 10 and you have 490 potential techniques, just from this viewpoint. Let's not talk about what happens when you examine 490 techniques from eight potential directions of the compass. And we won't even think about what happens when you start making combinations out of the 10 Baps (100) times eight directions (64) times the 490 potential techniques we just discussed (3,136,000 potential techniques).

And, truth be told, this is just one way of looking at the whole picture.

22 LINE EIGHT

1) Step back with the right foot to a Cat Stance as you cross the wrists in front of the body with the palms up.

2) Step forward with the left foot to a Toe Up Back Stance as you execute a Double Knife Block.

3) Retract the left foot to a Cat Stance as you execute a left Buddha Palm Block.

4) Execute a left Front Snap Kick.

5) Step forward with the left foot to a Toe Up Back Stance.

6) Shift forward into a Front Stance as you execute a right Punch.

7) Step forward with the right foot to a Cat Stance as you cross the wrists in front of the body with the palms up.

8) Step forward with the right foot to a Toe Up Back Stance as you execute a Double Knife Block.

9) Retract the right foot to a Cat Stance as you execute a right Cross Palm Block.

10) Execute a right Front Snap Kick.

11) Step forward with the right foot to a Toe Up Back Stance.

12) Shift forward into a Front Stance as you execute a left Punch.

13) Step forward with the left foot to a Cat Stance as you cross the wrists in front of the body with the palms up.

14) Step forward with the left foot to a Toe Up Back Stance as you execute a Double Knife Block.

15) Retract the left foot to a Cat Stance as you execute a left Buddha Palm Block.

16) Execute a left Front Snap Kick.

17) Step forward with the left foot to a Toe Up Back Stance.

18) Step forward with the left foot to a Front Stance as you execute a right Punch.

19) Step back with the left foot and face to the right in an Hourglass Stance as you execute a left Buddha Palm Block.

Pivot to the right and repeat the form in the opposite direction.

Special note:

True strength is measured in how many friends you have.

APPLICATION EIGHT

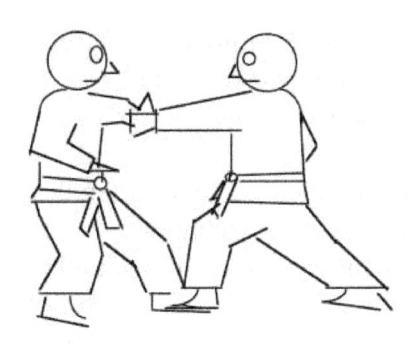

Wrist Twist: After palm block reach over opponent's hand with your blocking hand, grab his hand and turn over. Use other hand. Both thumbs point up to his middle knuckle and finger from both hands in the center of his palm. Walk backwards and lower him to the ground gently.

Can you make four more applications for two strike attacks, using the Buddha Palm Block first, then each of the basic blocks?

WARNING!
Be very gentle in twisting the wrist and lowering your partner to the ground!

23
CUTTING THE ART DOWN TO SIZE

So...over 3 million techniques, right. If it only took me ten minutes to learn each technique it would only take 30 million minutes, or 60 years. If I didn't sleep or eat.

Maybe we better rethink this.

The other guy has two arms and two legs. You can handle each attack from two sides, so that makes eight techniques.

And there you have it, there are only about eight workable techniques in each Art. Of course there will be three or four follow ups or variations, so make it 32 techniques per Art. If you learn four Arts you should be pretty well based. So over 20 or 30 years, if you are a dedicated Martial Artist, you should learn at least four Arts, and know about 120 techniques.

So go ahead and figure out the math so you can understand the scope of Art, but isolate the basic techniques that work, and concentrate on those.

Want to know something funny?

Take the 10 BAPs and figure out the main footwork behind an Art, and there are all your techniques.

The long and the short of it is if you can figure out what I mean your Art will be spectacular in a couple of years, not 20 or 30.

So how well do you analyze?

24
LINE NINE ~ THE SWORD CATCHER

1) Step back with the right foot into a Cat Stance Stance as you execute an open hand Crossed Wrist High Block. The left wrist should be in front.

2) Step forward with the left foot into a Toe Up Back Stance as you roll the left arm under the right arm. Execute a left Vertical Backfist as you retract the right hand.

3) Shift forward into a Front Stance as you execute a right Punch.

4) Step forward with the right foot into a Cat Stance as you execute a Crossed High Block. The right wrist should be in front.

5) Step forward with the right foot into a Toe Up Back Stance as you roll the right arm under the left arm. Execute a right Vertical Backfist as you retract the left hand.

6) Shift forward into a Front Stance as you execute a left Punch.

7) Step forward with the left foot into a Cat Stance Stance as you execute a Crossed Wrist High Block. The left wrist should be in front.

8) Step forward with the left foot into a Toe Up Back Stance as you roll the left arm under the right arm. Execute a left Vertical Backfist as you retract the right hand.

9) Shift forward into a Front Stance as you execute a right Punch.

10) Step back with the left foot and face to the right in an Hourglass Stance as you execute a left Buddha Palm Block.

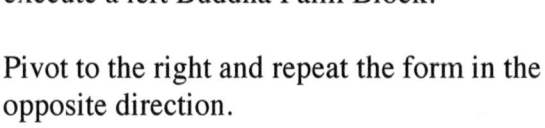

Pivot to the right and repeat the form in the opposite direction.

Special note:

To make this technique work pull on the wrist with the right hand and push up on the elbow with the left hand (this creates a 'Crank.') See following illustration.

APPLICATION NINE

APPLICATION TEN

What if you do the technique on the wrong side? Simply pull with the left hand and execute a right Outward Block, then punch with the left hand.

If he braces or holds on how could you use your knees? Elbows?

25
HOW TO PRESERVE THE TRUE ART

The reasons Karate, and other Martial Arts, become so warped out of true are varied.

Let's take one example.

Gichin Funakoshi taught Karate to school children in Okinawa. He undoubtedly changed the Art to make mass consumption easier, and to appeal to the needs of children.

Funakoshi then brought Karate from Okinawa to Japan in the 1920's. Undoubtedly there were problems of language. He also had to deal with the fact that he was teaching people of a different station in life.

After World War II American servicemen brought Karate to America, further fostering problems of linguistic translation and culture.

More alteration to tailor the Art to fit the needs of commercialism and real mass consumption.

Can you see the potential for alteration here? Even if one were to consider Funakoshi right.

Don't get me wrong, Funakoshi did wonderful and astounding things in his lifetime, bringing an Art to an entire world. But there are more variations of his Art than one could shake a skunk at. And this is in less than 100 years. The Art has actually had thousands and thousands of years to become altered.

The real key is that the True Art is rediscovered continuously. It is rediscovered through the simple process of Body Testing.

Body Testing allows you to actually look at the Art, to analyze it in real terms, and to understand what works and what doesn't work.

Even if everything I did was lost, somebody somewhere would start Body Testing and, therefore, rediscover everything all over again.

Thus, the True Art will prevail over the nature of the beast.

26
LINE TEN ~ THE FOOT CATCHER

1) Step back with the right foot into a Cat Stance Stance as you execute an open hand Crossed Wrist Low Block. The right wrist should be in front.

2) Step forward with the left foot into a Toe Up Back Stance as you execute a left Inward Block as you retract the right hand.

3) Shift forward into a Front Stance as you execute a right Punch.

4) Step forward with the right foot into a Cat Stance as you execute a Crossed Wrist Low Block. The left wrist should be in front.

5) Step forward with the right foot into a Toe Up Back Stance as you execute a right Inward Block.

6) Shift forward into a Front Stance as you execute a left Punch.

7) Step forward with the left foot into a Cat Stance Stance as you execute a Crossed Wrist Low Block. The right wrist should be in front.

8) Step forward with the left foot into a Toe Up Back Stance as you execute a left Inward Block.

10) Shift forward into a Front Stance as you execute a right Punch.

11) Step back with the left foot and face to the right in an Hourglass Stance as you execute a left Buddha Palm Block.
Pivot to the right and repeat the form in the opposite direction.

Special note:

To make this technique work pull the heel with the right hand and push on the foot with the left hand. Twine your hand as if wrist twisting.

APPLICATION ELEVEN

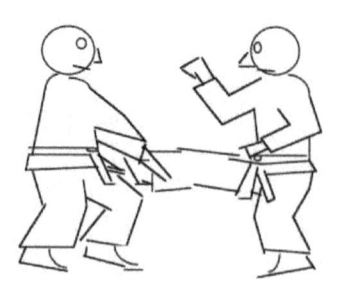

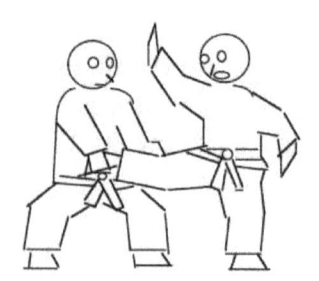

APPLICATION TWELVE

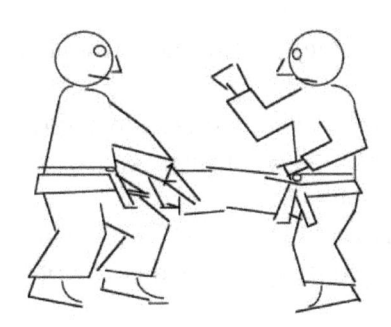

What if you can't catch the foot? It is easy to analyze what his next move is going to be.

Grab his right hand pull it to the left at the same time as you sweep his right foot to the right if you want a great Grab Art.

27
A SHAMELESS AD

I'm probably the only fellow doing any real research into the Art.

Everybody else is either memorizing what the old guys did, trying to figure out what has already been done, or just fighting.

What I am doing is understanding the Art.

This entails a study and comparison of methods. This means that I don't care about fighting, I care about rapid transmission of accurate data.

Speed and effectiveness, dude. We're light years ahead here.

28
LINE ELEVEN~ROLLING BACKFIST

1) Step back with the right foot into a Cat Stance Stance as you execute a left Buddha Palm Block.

2) Step forward with the left foot into a Toe Up Back Stance as you execute a left Low Block and a right High Block.

3) Retract the left foot into a Cat Stance as you execute a right Buddha Palm Block with a Dangling Forearm Block.

4) Roll the left fist inside to a Vertical Backfist as you Hook then retract the right fist as you execute a left Front Snap Kick.

5) Step forward with the left foot into a Front Stance as you execute a right Punch.

6) Step forward with the right foot into a Cat Stance Stance as you execute a right Buddha Palm Block.

7) Step forward with the right foot into a Toe Up Back Stance as you execute a right Low Block and a left High Block.

8) Retract the right foot into a Cat Stance as you execute a left Buddha Palm Block with a right Dangling Forearm.

9) Roll the right fist inside to a Vertical Backfist as you Hook then retract the left fist as you execute a right Front Snap Kick.

10) Step forward with the right foot into a Front Stance as you execute a left Punch.

11) Step forward with the left foot into a Cat Stance Stance as you execute a left Buddha Palm Block.

12) Step forward with the left foot into a Toe Up Back Stance as you execute a left Low Block and a right High Block.

13) Retract the left foot into a Cat Stance as you execute a right Buddha Palm Block with a left Dangling Forearm Block.

14) Roll the left fist inside to a Vertical Backfist as you Hook then retract the right fist as you execute a left Front Snap Kick.

15) Step forward with the left foot into a Front Stance as you execute a right Punch.

16) Step back with the left foot and face to the right in an Hourglass Stance as you execute a left Buddha Palm Block.

Pivot to the right and repeat the form in the opposite direction.

Special note:

Always look into the eyes. The eyes are the windows to a man's soul. It's like looking at a car that's aimed at you. If you look at the car you get hit. If you look at the person driving the car you will see what he is doing.

APPLICATION THIRTEEN

A slight side step to the right takes you off the line of attack and sets up the attacker's next strike, which makes him predictable.

If you place your left arm against the left (his) side of his head and push the left arm up and back the result is an Insertion Throw.

APPLICATION FOURTEEN

Slide the left hand underneath the block to grab and pull the Attacker's right hand. Drop the weight (into the right arm) by stomping the foot.

Can you use a horizontal elbow strike in this technique? A vertical elbow strike?

29
FIGHTING

Let's talk about fighting.

In True Karate one does not learn how to fight.

One learns how to scientifically analyze an opponent so that all 'What if's' are handleable.

If you are fighting then you aren't doing Karate.

This is true of any other Martial Art you may be practicing.

Fighting is chaos. Chaos is lacking data and the ability to use that data to resolve chaos.

When somebody wants to hit you they are trying to disorder you.

Anger in a wave, physical threat, all manner of things can be used to intimidate you. Your trick is to know your Art so well that you don't succumb to the wave of chaos, that you hang onto your knowledge of who and what you are, then reverse the flow, turning the chaos back to your attacker.

It all hinges upon staying aware and analytical.

It is not fighting.

It is scientifically rendering.

30
LINE TWELVE~FALLING CRANE

1) Step back with the right foot into a Cat Stance Stance as you execute a left Buddha Palm Block.

2) Hook the left foot behind the right knee in a Crane Stance as you execute a left Low Block and a right High Block.

3) Step forward with the left foot into a Toe Up Back Stance as you execute a right Buddha Palm Block.

4) Shift forward into a Front Stance as you execute a left Chop.

5) Execute a right Punch.

6) Step forward with the right foot into a Cat Stance Stance as you execute a right Buddha Palm Block.

7) Hook the right foot behind the left knee in a Crane Stance as you execute a right Low Block and a left High Block.

8) Step forward with the right foot into a Toe Up Back Stance as you execute a left Buddha Palm Block.

9) Shift forward into a Front Stance as you execute a right Chop.

10) Execute a left Punch.

11) Step forward with the left foot into a Cat Stance Stance as you execute a left Buddha Palm Block.

12) Hook the left foot behind the right knee in a Crane Stance as you execute a left Low Block and a right High Block.

13) Step forward with the left foot into a Toe Up Back Stance as you execute a right Buddha Palm Block.

14) Shift forward into a Front Stance as you execute a left Chop.

15) Execute a right Punch.

16) Step back with the left foot and face to the right in an Hourglass Stance as you execute a left Buddha Palm Block.

Pivot to the right and repeat the form in the opposite direction.

Special note:

If you work the line towards the North, crane the right knee to the Northwest and block the left hand to the Northeast.

APPLICATION FIFTEEN

You don't have to hook the Crane in this technique.

Side kicking is a good option.

Chop sideways, across the two dimensional plane of the feet. Push his knee out with your knee.

APPLICATION SIXTEEN

Be very careful when striking the knee. Allow your partner to twist and kneel so as to avoid injury. It only takes some fifteen pounds to break the knee at certain sideways angles.

Can you twist the head to effect a throw? Be careful with your partner.

31
MORE ABOUT FIGHTING

The secret of the Art is in the word 'Know.' To know one must look. To look one must go slow and look.

When I see freestyle being taught I cringe. People are being taught to lose 50% of the time.

On the other hand, if you go slow, looking at your opponent, and getting into the idea of your partner being somebody you want to teach and learn from, then you can take turns winning and losing without getting into a game where you learn to lose.

Really, it is assuming the viewpoint of the teacher.

If you are practicing any method of freestyle, or any of the related freestyle exercises, go slow and look, this is the secret of translating the True Art into reality .

32
LINE THIRTEEN ~ DART

1) Step back with the right foot into a Cat Stance as you execute a right Buddha Palm Block.

2) Step forward with the left foot into a Back Stance as you execute a left Low Block.

3) Shift forward into a Front Stance as you execute a right Punch.

4) Execute a right Oblique Foot Stomp.

5) Set the right foot down and bring the left foot up behind it in a Crossed Stance as you execute a left Punch and a right Upper Cross Palm Block.

6) Step back with the left foot into a Back Stance as you execute a right Low Block.

7) Shift forward into a Front Stance as you execute a left Punch.

8) Execute a left Oblique Foot Stomp.

9) Set the left foot down and bring the right foot up behind it in a Crossed Stance as you execute a right Punch and a left Upper Cross Palm Block.

10) Step back the right foot into a Back Stance as you execute a left Low Block.

11) Shift forward into a Front Stance as you execute a right Punch.

12) Execute a right Oblique Foot Stomp.

13) Set the right foot down and bring the left foot up behind it in a Crossed Stance as you execute a left Punch and a right Upper Cross Palm Block.
14) Step forward with the left foot and face to the right in an Hourglass Stance as you execute a left Buddha Palm Block.

Pivot to the right and repeat the form in the opposite direction.

Special note:

Do the following technique with the Low Block replaced with a High Block, then an Outward Block. What happens when you try to replace the Low Block with an Inward Block?

APPLICATION SEVENTEEN

APPLICATION EIGHTEEN

Move to the right, then pull the front foot back to make space for the foot stomp. when the attacker collapses hook the right arm and pull it.

Can you twist the head after the elbow strike?

33
THE MOST ABOUT FIGHTING

There are several important steps in learning how to Freestyle. These steps must be done so that the student is never intimidated and always learns to keep his awareness up.

Rhythmic Freestyle (Karate) Moving Position Force
Sticky Hands (Wing Chun) Fixed Position Force with Flow
Pushing Hands (Tai Chi)   Fixed Position Flow
One in Center (Aikido)   Moving Position Flow
One in Center disarms weapons expands concepts listed above.

There are other ways of understanding the sequence of teaching one how to freestyle.

Rhythmic Freestyle holds a position.
Sticky Hands holds a position while emptying the arms.
Pushing Hands holds a position while emptying the body.
One in the Center gives up a position while emptying the body.
One in Center Disarming expands spacial concepts of above.

And there are other types of freestyle. Most of the others are exercises which can be used to help a student understand the above, and the relation of the above. In the end one should be able to analyze the Force and Flow of any attack, and use his choice of Force or Flow in dealing with that attack.

34
LINE FOURTEEN ~ HAMMER

1) Step back with the right foot into a Cat Stance as you execute a right Buddha Palm Block with a left Dangling Forearm Block.

2) Step forward with the left foot into a Back Stance as you execute a left Outward Block and a right Low Block.

3) Execute a right Outward Block and a left Low Block.

4) Pivot into a Horse Stance as you execute a left Horizontal Elbow Strike to your right palm.

5) Execute a left Hammerfist.

6) Pivot into a Front Stance as you execute a right Punch.

7) Step forward with the right foot into a Back Stance as you execute a right Outward Block and a left Low Block.

8) Execute a left Outward Block and a right Low Block.

9) Pivot into a Horse Stance as you execute a right Horizontal Elbow Strike to your left palm.

10) Execute a right Hammerfist.

11) Pivot into a Front Stance as you execute a left Punch.

12) Step forward with the left foot into a Back Stance as you execute a left Outward Block and a right Low Block.

13) Execute a right Outward Block and a left Low Block.

14) Pivot into a Horse Stance as you execute a left Horizontal Elbow Strike to the left palm.

15) Execute a left Hammerfist.

16) Pivot into a Front Stance as you execute a right Punch.

17) Step forward with the left foot and face to the right in an Hourglass Stance as you execute a left Buddha Palm Block.

Pivot to the right and repeat the form in the opposite direction.

Special note:

When you strike somebody pretend you are knocking on a door. Make the most noise in the house for the least amount of effort in the knuckles. Feel the Energy build in the Tan Tien, course out the structure to explode in the fist. (It's a whiplike sensation!)

APPLICATION NINETEEN

Simultaneous left outward middle block and right low block.

Simultaneous right outward middle block and left low block. Groin Strike optional.

Left horizontal elbow strike followed by Left elbow spike.

Apply your techniques to somebody striking with a weapon.

APPLICATION TWENTY

This is called an Insertion Throw. If the attacker is taller you may have to place your arm under his arm, instead of against his neck. Be prepared to execute 'Shock and Lock' techniques to make this work. Be prepared to walk in a circle behind your attacker.

Can you make other lines? Can you explore techniques from other Arts and change them into Buddha Crane Lines? How many more applications can you find in the lines I have shown you?

35
THE GEOMETRY OF THE ARTS

Leonardo DaVinci is said to have arrived at a city after the outer gates were closed.

'But I'm Leonardo DaVinci!' protested the famous Artist.

'Prove it,' said the gatekeeper.

So Leonardo drew a perfect circle, freehand, on the gates of the city.

The gatekeeper, convinced because of the difficulty of drawing a perfect circle freehand, let DaVinci enter the city.

Art is geometry. It is the visualization of something geometrically perfect, and the execution of that perfect visualization into the 'Real world.'

Remember, as you explore Buddha Crane Karate, that if you draw a Perfect Geometry you will enter the Art.

36
HOUSE

House is the basic Form, the first real sentence after learning the 'Words' of the 'Lines.' When doing House one develops straight line Intention. One can also find extra techniques if they read between the moves.

1) From a Natural Stance pivot to the left and retract the left leg into a Cat Stance as you execute a left Buddha Palm Block.

2) Step forward with the left leg into a Back Stance as you execute a left Low Block.

3) Step forward with the left leg as you execute a right Punch.

4) Step forward with the right leg into a Cat Stance as you execute a left Buddha Palm Block with a right dangling Forearm Block.

5) Step forward with the right leg into a Back Stance as you execute a right Outward Middle Block.

6) Step forward with the right leg into a Front Stance as you execute a Punch.

7) Step forward with the left leg into a Cat Stance as you execute a right Buddha Palm Block.

8) Step forward with the left leg into a Back Stance as you execute a left High Block.

9) Step forward with the left leg into a Front Stance as you execute a right Punch.

10) Step back with the left leg (facing to the side) into an Hourglass Stance as you execute a left Buddha Palm Block.

SPECIAL NOTE:

It is fun and enlightening to apply Buddha Palm concepts to classical forms. Forms analyzed through the Buddha Palm Method become much more understandable and usable.

37
TWO MAN HOUSE

Blocking Exercises are very important. They teach timing, toughen up the arms, give technique additional reality, increase potential for further understanding, change appreciations of angles, and so on.

This exercise can be done a variety of different ways. If you look at it closely you will understand that it is nothing more than the first three lines of Buddha Crane. The fact of the matter is that every line can be translated into a Two Man Blocking Exercise. And there is an unending potential for creation of further exercises as you learn to 'Mix and match' the lines of Buddha Crane.

Attacker A steps forward with the right foot as he executes a left Punch to the groin.

Defender B steps back with the left foot as he executes a right Low Block.

Attacker A steps forward with the left foot as he executes a right Punch to the chest.

Defender B steps back with the right foot as he executes a right Outward Middle Block.

Attacker A steps forward with the right foot as he executes a left Punch to the face.

Defender B steps back with the left foot as he executes a right High Block.

The Defender becomes the Attacker, the Attacker becomes the Defender.

Attacker B (on the right) shifts forward with the right foot and punches to the chest with the left hand. Defender A will commence blocking and moving backward to Attacker B's attacks.

Execute the sequence in the other direction with the left and right directions reversed.

38
MOON

The Form Moon has gone through some interesting translations. There are variations in Japanese, Okinawan and Chinese Martial Arts. Among the names are Hangetsu and Seisan.

The version I offer here is a simple version. The purpose is to teach the student to properly sink his weight while executing simple blocks. Extensive Body Testing should be used on this form. Beginning students should be pushed. Advanced students should have the arms resisted extensively. Expert students should be struck with much Force. If you are getting this Form out of this book for the first time and have no experience in striking students then I suggest you get some proper instruction before doing so. There is a precise science to the striking of students, and if you don't know it you could damage them.

I always tell students to 'Stand like a mountain,' when I am teaching them this Form.

From a Natural Stance take a right Moon Step (semi~circular) to an Hourglass Stance. When the right foot is in the left hand should be in a Buddha Palm position with the right hand dangling. When the right foot is out sink the weight and emphasize a right Outward Middle Block.

Take a left Moon Step (semi~circular) to an Hourglass Stance. When the left foot is in the right hand should be in a Buddha Palm position with the left hand dangling. When the left foot is out sink the weight and emphasize a left Outward Middle Block.

Take a right Moon Step (semi~circular) to an Hourglass Stance. When the right foot is in the left hand should be in a Buddha Palm position with the right hand dangling. When the right foot is out sink the weight and emphasize a right Outward Middle Block.

Circle the hands outwards and execute a double Parry. Follow the Double Parry with a double Foreknuckle Strike to the front. Make sure the weight sinks and sinks and sinks.

Standing in place execute a High Crossed Wrist Block. Follow this Crossed Wrist Block with Double Low Blocks to the sides.

At this point step across the left foot with the right foot into an Hourglass Stance facing the other direction. Don't forget to guard the face with the right Cross Palm when you turn. As you sink your weight execute a left Outward (palm up) Outward Block and a right (palm down) Low Block. Do the next move as if encountering extreme tension! Bring the left hand in and down in a 'Half moon' arc to a Low Block. At the same time bring the right hand in and up in a 'Half moon' arc to an Outward Block. While the form is facing back the way it came, the viewpoint of illustration changes 180 degrees at this point.

Take a Half Moon Step with the right foot into an Hourglass Stance as you execute a right Outward (palm up) Middle Block and a left (palm down) Low Block. Do the next move as if encountering extreme tension! Bring the right hand in and down in a 'Half moon' arc to a Low Block. At the same time bring the left hand in and up in a 'Half moon' arc to an Outward Block.

Take a Half Moon Step with the left foot into an Hourglass Stance as you execute a left Outward (palm up) Middle Block and a right (palm down) Low Block. Do the next move as if encountering extreme tension! Bring the left hand in and down in a 'Half moon' arc to a Low Block. At the same time bring the right hand in and up in a 'Half moon' arc to an Outward Block.

Circle the hands outwards and execute a double Parry. Follow the Double Parry with a double Foreknuckle Strike to the front. Make sure the weight sinks and sinks and sinks.

Standing in place execute a High Crossed Wrist Block. Follow this Crossed Wrist Block with Double Low Blocks to the sides.

Step across the left foot with the right foot to the beginning position to end the Form.

39
VISION OF THE WHITE CRANE

Gichin Funakoshi, the founder of Modern Karate, the man most responsible for the spread of Karate throughout the world, wrote that one should study a single Form for many years. Later in his writings he stated that he had been having second thoughts about practicing in such a manner.

He was right the first time. He should have had no doubts. Yet it is hard not to have doubts when one is offered such a smorgasbord of technique and training in these modern days.

I recommend to the young student that he learn as much as possible from whoever he can, then isolate a couple of Forms to concentrate on. I recommend that while he should practice whatever he learns until he thoroughly understands it, he should pick his favorite Forms and spend his life concentrating on them.

Learning a lot of different Forms gives breadth. Concentrating on a few Forms gives depth. One needs breadth of technique so that he will not be fooled by something he has not seen. One needs depth of technique so that he will have the ability to make it work.

I practiced many types of Karate for many years before I selected the exact Forms I wished to concentrate on. I had to do much research before I possessed the exact Forms that would do me the most good.

In selecting this Form you are about to learn I searched for the most common and most useful techniques. I tried many different ways of arranging the material, creating whole series of Forms and Arts in my searchings. I paid particular attention to the manifestation of Energy and Concept, for such is the root of True Art.

The Form you are about to learn is called 'The Vision of the White Crane,' or, simply , 'Crane.'

It is a Form which teaches Power and Grace, balance and technique, peace of mind and how to destroy an opponent.

While one can practice this Form with the 'Loose~tight' method of closing the fists for internal Power, I prefer to practice it with open hands. I also practice all the earlier lines with open hands. Of course I have been practicing long enough that I have power in my fists, and wish to extend that power to my fingertips. This is something you can think about over the next decade or two

CAMERA ANGLES WILL VARY TO PRESENT THE BEST VIEWPOINT OF THE MOVEMENT BEING PRESENTED. TO AVOID CONFUSION FOLLOW THE FOOT PATTERN.

1) From a Natural Stance facing north step to the right into a Horse Stance. Execute a left Low Knife Block, both palms to face down. Drop the full body weight into the block and pretend you are slicing through infinity .

2) Execute a right Outward Middle Knife Block. Both palms are facing up.
Stay in the Horse Stance and keep the weight down, thus making the Tan Tien (body generator) create more Energy .

The Energy Formula:
Weight = Work = Energy

3) Execute a left High Knife Block. The left palm is edge to the eyes. The right palm is face up.

EXERCISE

Repeat steps 1~3 alternating sides. See how many counts you can do. It is not important to count fast, but rather to count approx. one move per second, and to ridge the Energy correctly in the arms. If you concentrate on focus in blocking you will not perceive pain in the legs. Remember: 'Think about pain and you get pain. Think about what you are doing and you will get what you are doing.' This is the Secret of Superior Intention.

3a) Move the left hand down to a Buddha Palm Block. Create 'Unbendable Arms.'

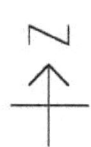

4) Pivot to the right into a Back Stance as you circle the right hand to a right Middle Knife Block. The left palm should guard the face on the way down and end up facing in to the Tan Tien.

    The arc of the block should be diagonal so that both hip rotation and body weight can be put into the movement.

5a) Execute a left Spearhand. Make sure you turn the left hip into the strike.
The three elements of Power are: Thrusting, weight dropping and hip rotation. These are the X, Y and Z of Karate Power. Figure out how to combine all three in each technique and you will unleash your Intention.

5b) Bring the left foot up to the right and pivot 135 degrees to the left. You should be facing to the Northwest. The left hand should be straight out and the knees bent.

Straighten the knees as you retract the left arm.

6a) Step forward (Northwest) with the left foot into a Front Stance as you protect the face from the side with a right Buddha Palm Block.

The Form is actually done on a square, or a diamond. This gives elementary knowledge concerning fighting to the front, angles and sides.

6b) Assume a Crane Stance on the left leg with the right foot hooked behind the knee. Simultaneously execute a right Low Block and a left High Block.
You should be able to hold this position as long as you wish with your eyes closed.

7a) Extend the right foot in a Toe Up Back Stance (Northeast) as you protect the face with the left palm and cup the elbow with the right hand.

One option is to move slow, thus gaining awareness and 'Suspensive Strength.'

7b) Step forward (Northeast) with the right foot into a Front Stance as you execute a right horizontal Chop.

Fingers to toes, shoulders and hips, should be one aligned curve.

7c) Execute a left Spear. Use hips for power.

Practice push ups on hands, fists, forefingers, two fingers, one finger (straight!).

Focus your mind to balance the finger bones.

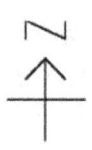

8a) Protect the face from the side with a right Buddha Palm Block.

While there are 'Whipping motions' with the hands one must search for the perfect circles of geometry.

N

8b) Assume a Crane Stance on the right leg with the left foot hooked behind the knee. Simultaneously execute a left Low Block and a right High Block.

You can create dynamic tension with the foot and then let slip to a kick. This will build explosive strength.

9a) Extend the left foot in a Toe Up Back Stance (Northwest) as you protect the face with the right palm and cup the elbow with the left hand.

A Toe Up Back Stance can be a Stomp to an Attacker's knee.

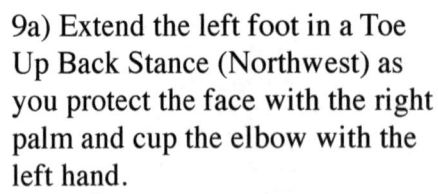

9b) Step forward (Northwest) with the left foot into a Front Stance as you execute a left horizontal Chop.

    I call this 'Opening the joint.' Pretend the hinge is the left shoulder and left hip.

9c) Execute a right Spear. Use hips for power.

    Breath out when you strike. Breathe out when you get struck. Always breathe from the Tan Tien.

10a) Step forward with the right foot (North) into a Back Stance as you execute a right Low Block and a left High Block.

    The camera angle has been changed 90 degrees to clarify posture.

    Make sure you circle the right hand counterclockwise. This can be a parry.

10b) Pivot in place 90 degrees to left (West) into an Hourglass Stance as you execute a left Buddha Palm Block.

    One must hold the 'Ground' through all motions, transitional or not.

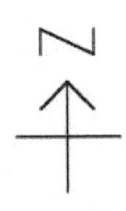

10c) Pivot in place 180 degrees (South) as you execute a left Low Block and right High Block. Camera angle is still 90 degrees.
Guard the face with the left hand then cross the hands as you make the transition from 10A to 10B.

10a) Right Back Stance
10b) Right Toe In to Hourglass Stance
10c) Left Toe Out to Left Back Stance

This diagram represents the footwork for movement number 10A to 10B. Pivoting should be done on the heels. Practice it until nobody can see the individual parts of the movement.

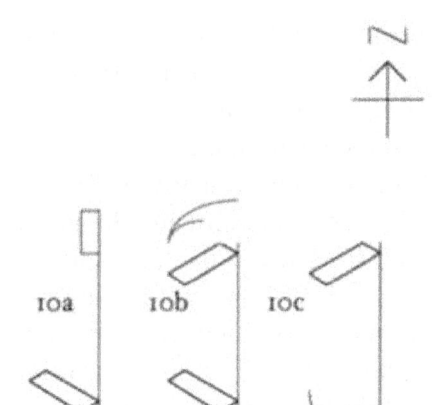

11a) Draw the left foot back to a Cat Stance (Southeast) as you turn the right foot to the South and execute a left Buddha Palm Block.
    Don't forget, the Buddha Palm Slap is the first instinctive motion one makes on being attacked. Don't untrain it...use it!

11b) Step forward to the Southeast into a Front Stance as you execute a right Low Block and a left High Block. Front Stance faces Southeast, Low Block to the Southwest
    Camera angle is still 90 degrees.
    In all stances there is a triangle with the Tan Tien as the peak and the feet as the base. The Tan Tien should never go outside the base of the feet.

12a) Bring the right foot forward until it is next to the left foot as you pivot (Southwest) and assume a Cat Stance. Simultaneously guard the face with the right palm and the groin with the back of the left hand.
    Most fights will not happen from the front, but from the side, or rear. This is just the cowardly nature of the attacking beast.

12b) Execute a right Front Snap kick, a left Parry (Hook), and a right Vertical Backwrist. (Southwest)
    Align your body properly and you will find the alignment of the next move happening naturally. This should be true of every Form. Toss out excessive preparation and chambering and you will find an efficient and fight oriented form.

12c) Step forward (Southwest) with the right foot into a Front Stance as you execute a left Horizontal elbow to the right Palm.
    It is easier to put the body weight behind an elbow .

13) Without moving the hips execute a left Low Block and a right High Block. The Stance is Southwest and the Block is Southeast.

Instead of using the hips for power rely on the explosion in the Tan Tien and channel to the cutting hand. After a few thousand cuts you will realize your internal power.

14a) Retract the left foot until it is next to the right foot as you pivot (southeast) and assume a Cat Stance. Simultaneously guard the face with the left palm and the groin with the back of the right hand.

Back up a couple of inches and the attacker's arm will reach it's limit and start to circle. This is a major opening for Grab Arts if you can move forward.

14b) Execute a left Front Snap kick, a right Parry (Hook), and a left Vertical Backwrist. (Southeast)

Stand on one leg and kick to the four corners 250 times per leg per kick.

123

14c) Step forward (Southeast) with the left foot into a Front Stance as you execute a right Horizontal elbow to the left Palm.

    Slapping the elbow toughens it as well as giving a sense of timing to the move.

15) Pivot a little over 180 degrees to beginning Horse Stance position. Chop to the right. Left arm is square in front of the body.

    You must see the Thought before the Action for this move to work properly. The exact concept deals with exploding the Tan Tien.

    Return the right foot to the Natural Stance to end the Form.

SPECIAL NOTE:

    The secret of Mastering the Martial Arts is countless repetition. Do a technique a 1000 times and you will be Expert (Black Belt). Do it 3,000 times and you will be Master. Do it 10,000 times and you will know it. In the Martial Arts this is the supreme truth.

40
THE SECRET OF THE WHITE CRANE

The Secret of the White Crane is captured in footwork and Form potentials.

If you look at the footwork you will see the eight directions of the compass.

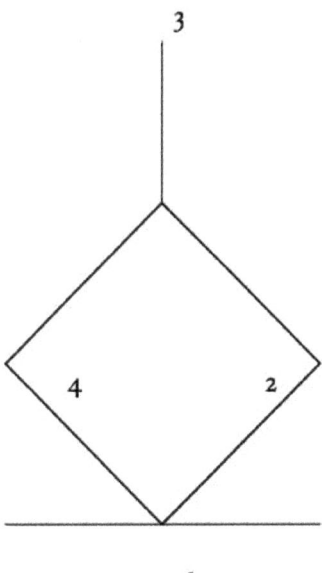

1 and 5

Lines 1, 3 and 5 will always stay the same. These are counts 1~5 of the Form, count 10, and count 15.

But sections 2 and 4, which are counts 6~9 and 11~14 of the Form, change.

Sections 2 and 4 can have any of the lines substituted. For instance, start with the Horse Stance and blocks, do a line on the zig zag up. Do the Back Stance White Crane 180 degree direction change, then do a line on the zig zag back. End with the Replacement Hammer Horse.

Which lines you use are up to you. You can even split the lines up and back further and use four lines.

And if you are clever you may find usable line alterations. Make sure they are usable, though.

You may have to jiggle the footwork slightly .

Thus the one Form can become 64 Forms, (1 of 8 lines up times 1 of 8 lines back) or more.

41
EXTRA APPLICATIONS

It is very important to concentrate on the Applications already listed. One should, however, make sure that they understand all the ramifications and potentials, that they can 'Read between the lines.' Thus I recommend practicing the following variations.

The above three blocks utilize variations of Stance on the basic blocks.

These moves are from counts 1~3 of the Form.

SPECIAL NOTE:
The power of a punch is measured by weight transferred to another object. Therefore:

$$Velocity \times Weight = Impact$$

Many people get so carried away with striking they forget that the Art is a matter of control. The above technique starts you on the road to control by teaching you to 'Manhandle' an opponent without respect for his wishes. This move is from counts 4~5 of the Form.

In addition to forgetting that they must rudely move an opponent around, people forget that they can move around. The above technique illustrates how one can use the footwork of the Form to move around an opponent. This technique is from count 6a of the Form.

One should start compiling sequences of techniques so that collapsing ranges, which are a very real possibility in a fight, can be handled. This means kick to punch to knee to elbow to throw, the five distances, are controlled easily . This technique is from count 6b of the Form.

Note the potential for a knee stomp. It's good technique to force the opponent's knee outward. (Or inward if he has narrowed his stance too much.)

The secret of this technique is in the timing. This is not merely a block and counter technique, but one where you have to block in between the precise movements of a normal block and counter technique.

Another example of collapsing distance. Don't forget about the potential of the foot stomp. This technique is from count 6b~7c.

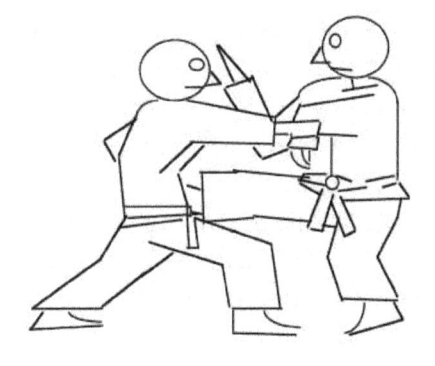

This technique teaches one how to control an opponent and thus set him up for follow up after follow up. A simple twist of the head and he will be on the ground with a broken neck. This technique is from counts 11b~12c.

Explode from the Tan Tien turn to the left 270 degrees into a Horse Stance as you execute a left Chop to the throat. A Hammerfist to the mid section is great, too.

Note: in the beginning you may take a cheat step backwards with the left foot. Eventually you must perform the following movement with no cheat step.

Once you understand this technique you will understand how CBM is a purity of explosion wherein the body keeps pace with the wave of expanding (directed) Energy. Normally it is not a good idea to turn one's back on an opponent.

The secret of this technique is to see it happen in your mind. To visualize it happening, then to relax and let it happen. The success of this technique depends upon you seeing the Thought behind the Action.

This technique is from count 15 of the Form.

Instead of chopping, or hammering, try kicking when you spin. Make sure you don't circle or unduly arc the kick. The success of this technique depends on being efficient in your path from the ground to the attacker's stomach.

Make sure your feet start at the same time, and end at the same time (hit the ground and hit the opponent simultaneously.)

Don't do this technique with a partner unless you have excellent control!

This is a variation on count 15 of the Form.

SPECIAL NOTE:

There are many other variations, deviations, potentials, and so on in this Form. You will find that time will reveal them. Are you willing to invest the time? Remember, what you find in the Form is what you find in yourself.

42
THE FINAL WORD

The final word is:

Analyze and Handle all Forms of Force and Flow and you will Master the Martial Arts.

Control yourself on all levels and you will find that your life is your own.

CBM your life and you will get what you want out of life.

Seek the True Art and you will find that You are the True Art.

About the Author

Al Case walked into his first martial arts school in 1967. During the Gold Age of Martial Arts he studied such arts as Aikido, Wing Chun, Ton Toi Northern Shaolin, Fut Ga Southern Shaolin, Weapons, Tai Chi Chuan, Pa Kua Chang, and others.

In 1981 he began writing for the martial arts magazines, including Inside Karate, Inside Kung Fu, Black Belt, Masters and Styles, and more.

In 1991 he was asked to write his own column in Inside Karate.

Beginning in 2001 he completed the basic studies of Matrixing, a logic approach to the Martial Arts he had been working on for over 30 years.

2011 he was heavily immersed in creating Neutronics, the science behind the science of Matrixing.

Interested martial artists can avail themselves of his research into Matrixing at MonsterMartialArts.com.

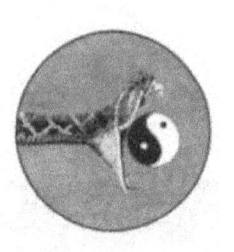

MonsterMartialArts.com

Did you know...

Al Case has written over forty novels?
Go to:

AlCaseBooks.com

AL CASE

Matrixing Kenpo Karate Series!

Matrixing Kenpo Karate
Book One
THE REAL HISTORY
Al Case

Matrixing Kenpo Karate
Book Two
THE SECRET OF FORMS
Al Case

Matrixing Kenpo Karate
Book Three
CREATING A NEW KENPO
Al Case

Pre~Matrixing Series

PAN GAI NOON KARATE/KUNG FU
Book One: Pre-Matrixing Martial Arts Encyclopedia
Al Case

KANG DUK WON KOREAN KARATE
Book Two: Pre-Matrixing Martial Arts Encyclopedia
Al Case

KWON BUP AMERICAN KARATE
Book Three: Pre-Matrixing Martial Arts Encyclopedia
Al Case

OUTLAW KARATE BEYOND TRADITIONAL
Book Four: Pre-Matrixing Martial Arts Encyclopedia
Al Case

BUDDHA CRANE KARATE
Book Five: Pre-Matrixing Martial Arts Encyclopedia
Al Case

MARTIAL ARTS BOOKS
On the internet

Advanced Tai Chi Chuan for Real Self Defense!
Black Belt Yoga
Five Martial Arts!
The Last Martial Arts Book (w video links!)
Hidden Techniques of Karate (w video links!)
How to Fix Karate (book one) (w video links!)
How to Fix Karate (book two) (w video links!)
Matrixing Kenpo Karate: Creating a New Kenpo
Matrixing Kenpo Karate: The Real History
Matrixing Kenpo Karate: The Secret of Forms
Neutropia ~ Surrealistic Poetry
The Book of Matrixing
The Book of Neutronics

VIDEO INSTRUCTION
DVDs and downloads at MonsterMartialArts.com

Matrix Karate
Matrix Kung Fu
Matrix Aikido
Master Instructor Course
Shaolin Butterfly
Butterfly Pa Kua Chang
Matrix Tai Chi Chuan
Five Army Tai Chi Chuan
Matrix Tai Chi Chuan
Five Army Tai Chi Chuan
Matrixing Kenjutsu
Blinding Steel (Matrixing Weapons)

Milton Keynes UK
Ingram Content Group UK Ltd.
UKHW022127051124
450708UK00015B/1213